RESTING IN HIM

RESTING IN HIM

Margaret Feinberg

Foreword by Patsy Clairmont

THOMAS NELSON
Since 1798

NASHVILLE   DALLAS   MEXICO CITY   RIO DE JANEIRO   BEIJING

Published in Nashville, Tennessee, by Thomas Nelson. Thomas Nelson is a registered trademark of Thomas Nelson, Inc.

Thomas Nelson, Inc. titles may be purchased in bulk for educational, business, fund-raising, or sales promotional use. For information, please e-mail SpecialMarkets@ThomasNelson.com.

Scripture quotations are taken from *The Holy Bible*, New International Version®. NIV®. © 1973, 1978, 1984 by International Bible Society. Used by permission of Zondervan. All rights reserved.

Scripture quotations marked NKJV are taken from *The Holy Bible,* The New King James Version® (NKJV). © 1979, 1980, 1982, 1992, Thomas Nelson, Inc., Publishers.

ISBN 978-1-4185-2938-3

Printed in China

09 10 11 12 RRD 9 8 7 6 5 4

Contents

Contents

Foreword

Screech!

It's okay. Really. It's just me slamming on my brakes in the midst of a whirlwind schedule. Honestly, I had to giggle when I was asked to greet you at the opening of a study called *Resting In Him*. Then I thought that perhaps this was a heavenly plot to slow me down (again), and that maybe, just maybe, some of my girlfriends needed to join me. I wouldn't be surprised if you can relate.

Go ahead, hit your brakes . . . take a deep breath. Now doesn't that feel better even for a moment?

Opportunities in life abound! They always have, and they always will, but here's the kicker: when given the chance, busyness will eat us for lunch. We were not meant to do all that is before us, as admirable as it might sound. Doing too much will strip our gears and drain our energy tank. Then we become a sputtering list of excuses as to why we are tardy, or speeding, or unable to make deadlines, or unprepared, and the list goes on. But the worst part is when we try to maintain a performance-based lifestyle, because doing so will either wad our nerves into an explosive bundle or gradually shut down legitimate emotions, leaving us numb. And one more thing a crammed lifestyle will do is convince us that we are only as valuable as what we can achieve in a day. Then when we are not smokin' our productivity tires, we feel guilty.

I love a sense of accomplishment. I celebrate what looks like progress in a project or in my personal growth, but I have learned along life's freeways that even good intentions can leave us harried if we have taken on more than we should have.

One year I sprung an exhaustion leak of such magnitude that I had to take a season off my speaking commitments and seek therapy just to find myself again under my relentless schedule.

It's not wrong to have a full life or even a busy agenda, but when it costs you or your family more than it should, it's time to re-evaluate. Life pacing is tricky because quite honestly some seasons will require more of us than others. But we have to make sure we are not trying to live out someone else's expectations for us, that we are not in a flurry just to indulge an unhealthy tendency to people-please, or that we haven't bought into the lie that we have no choice but to career through life at a breakneck pace.

Honestly, I could be the visual aid for this study because I have such a propensity to extremes (especially where rushing and running come in), so I am grateful for studies that remind us to slow down, think, and then proceed with holy caution.

So girlfriends, join an adrenalin-addicted junky as I sit in the shelter of the truth that I need to "Be still and know that He is God." For it is there that I calm down and settle into a Christ-led existence of sanity, focus, and purpose.

—Patsy Clairmont

Introduction

Rest for Your Soul

*The LORD replied, "My Presence will go with you,
and I will give you rest."*

—EXODUS 33:14

Rest. Our souls crave it. Our bodies demand it. Our spirits are renewed through it. Yet rest is one of those treasures that we often don't take the time to enjoy in the busyness of life. As the pace of our modern world speeds up, we find ourselves trying to do more in the same amount of time. Left unchecked, we become experts in efficiency— running hard and fast on the treadmill of life. Our souls grow weary. Our bodies grow weak. Our spirits run dry.

When asked what a person truly needs to survive, most people list air, water, and food, while forgetting that rest is also vitally important to our bodies, minds, and spirits. Rest has the power to transform our attitudes, our actions, and even our activities. When well-rested, we are better equipped to face the challenges as well as the occasional curveball daily life often throws at us.

Meanwhile, the God who formed and shaped us offers us rest—*real rest*—in Him. He invites us to step off the treadmill of life and discover the renewal and restoration that can only come from Him. When we take time to rest, we begin to realize that what feels like doing nothing is really allowing God to do something inside of us. Our souls are given a chance to renew. Our physical bodies are given a chance to heal. Our spirits are given the opportunity to connect with God. In those precious moments, we are reminded not just of who we are but whose we are. Afterward, we find ourselves echoing a common response, *I needed that!*

The ultimate rest you will ever experience doesn't just take place during a nap or a lazy Sunday afternoon. Instead, it's found in God. He is the One who renews your weary soul. He is the One who gives you strength when you think you can't go any farther—emotionally, physically, spiritually, and relationally. The rest that God provides is like no other. Don't you think it's time that you take a break and enter into the rest God has for you?

My hope and prayer is that through this study, you will discover real rest—the kind that God has specifically designed for you—and learn to relax in the arms of your Savior.

Blessings,
Margaret Feinberg

The Speed of Life

While every day has the exact same number of hours,

minutes, and seconds, it's amazing how fast some days

seem to go by! The first three lessons ask you to look at

the speed of your life and the importance of rest.

One

The Stress Test

I said, "Oh, that I had the wings of a dove!
I would fly away and be at rest."

—PSALM 55:6

Have you noticed all the time-savers available at your local grocery store? Prepackaged food promises to save you preparation and cooking time. Cleaning products claim that with a few quick squirts you'll never have to scrub again. When you approach the checkout, you can choose between the standard lane, the express lane, and the do-it-yourself lane—whichever is fastest for you!

One of the great ironies of the twenty-first century is that despite all the technological advances of time-saving devices, many people feel they're more time-crunched than ever before. For many, it feels like the pace of life has been steadily increasing—and with good reason. A recent study found that the average American now works a forty-six-hour workweek, and more than a third of those surveyed work more than fifty hours a week. That leaves less time to do chores, spend time with family and friends, and of course, rest.

At the same time, many people are feeling the effects of the time-crunch: stress. A recent survey on iVillage.com revealed that only half the people feel they are coping well with multitasking their lives—the other half are not. In fact, 47 percent—a majority of whom are women—said they are concerned with the level of stress in their lives.

Without much warning, the "To-Do List" of life can get pretty long—work, meetings, activities, family, carpooling, friends, exercise, shopping, chores—and can even seem overwhelming. Sometimes the stress in our lives manifests itself in our attitudes and responses to daily life. Just how stressed are you? Place a check mark by all the statements that describe you:

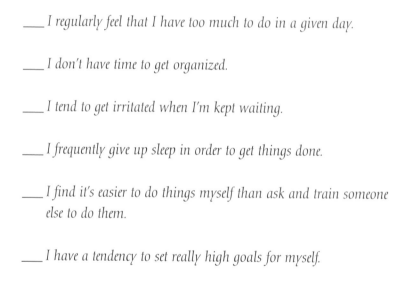

_____ *I regularly feel that I have too much to do in a given day.*

_____ *I don't have time to get organized.*

_____ *I tend to get irritated when I'm kept waiting.*

_____ *I frequently give up sleep in order to get things done.*

_____ *I find it's easier to do things myself than ask and train someone else to do them.*

_____ *I have a tendency to set really high goals for myself.*

If you checked more than two of the statements above, then you may have more stress in your life than you realized. No matter how overworked or overscheduled you've become, God desires to restore you. In fact, your level of exhaustion and need for rest will never match God's desire to give you rest. He longs to renew you! He invites you to step off the treadmill of life and find your rest in Him. This is the kind of rest that goes deeper than a good night's sleep or an afternoon at the spa; this is the rest that renews the innermost parts of your being and reminds you whose you are.

    1. What are some of your favorite time-saving devices or best practices for saving time?

    2. Have you ever purchased a time-saving device that actually took more time than it was worth? Describe.

Despite all the time-saving gadgets and practices in our modern world, many women feel more time-crunched than ever. The result of being overworked and overscheduled is often stress.

    3. On a scale of one to ten, how much stress do you feel you have in your life right now? Can you identify some of the sources of the stress in your life?

During Jesus' life He undoubtedly felt pressure and stress. Wherever Jesus went, people wanted something from Him—a healing, a teaching, a moment with Him. In the first chapter of the Gospel of Mark, we get a glimpse into Jesus' busy schedule.

   4. Read **Mark 1:21–34**. *In the space that follows make a list of all the things Jesus did in a very short amount of time.*

After all that Jesus did, His physical body must have been exhausted. Despite all the immediate needs, Jesus did something specific to handle the stress and pressure.

   5. Read **Mark 1:35**. *Why do you think this one activity was so crucial to Jesus' life and the impact He had on others?*

   6. *Why do you think finding solitary time to pray is important to your life and the impact you have on others?*

7. How does taking the time to get away to pray change you?

8. How does taking time to get away and pray enable you to handle the stress and pressures of life better? Is there anything that prevents you from getting away to pray more often?

The truth is that no matter how overworked or overscheduled you may feel, God desires to restore you. Your desire for rest will never match God's desire to give you rest. He longs to renew you!

Digging Deeper

On several occasions throughout the Gospels Jesus retreated to a solitary place. Read **Luke 4:42–43**. Why do you think Jesus chose a solitary place? One of the results of His time in this place was that He was more confident of His purpose (v. 43). How does spending time with Jesus make you more confident of your purpose?

Ponder and Pray

The opening Scripture for this lesson comes from **Psalm 55:6**, "I said, 'Oh, that I had the wings of a dove! I would fly away and be at rest.'" Have you ever wanted to "fly away" from a situation because of stress or exhaustion? Where do you tend to go when your soul desires rest? Are there any unhealthy places you're tempted to go? What kinds of healthy places can you choose instead?

Bonus Activity

Over the course of the next week, pay attention to any moments in which you feel stress. What are the causes? Are there any common sources of the stress you feel? Are there any areas in which you need to cut back, say "no," or make lifestyle changes in order to lessen the amount of stress in your life?

Two

The Benefits of Rest

*To whom he said, "This is the resting place, let the
weary rest"; and, "This is the place of repose"—
but they would not listen.*

—ISAIAH 28:12

During the Gold Rush, everyone wanted to get to California. There were two notable wagon trains that made the journey west. One was led by a Christian who believed it was important to stop every week to worship God and rest. The other leader took a different approach. He believed that the quickest way to strike gold was to go hard and never rest.

Though both wagons departed on the same day, do you know which wagon train arrived in California first? The one who chose to rest on the Lord's Day.

The power and benefits of rest cannot be understated. Everyone needs time to relax and recuperate. When denied this natural rhythm in life, you are more tempted to turn to unhealthy alternatives—including caffeine and sugar—for the energy you need. In addition, lack of rest decreases your ability to concentrate and increases irritability. You're more likely to be snappy or cranky when you're not well rested. When you're sleep-deprived, you're more likely to make mistakes and misspeak. Without enough sleep, your reaction time is also decreased—making you more susceptible to accidents.

On the flip side, rest may do more for you than you think. Rest is recognized to boost your immune system. Rest enables your body to ward off illness and disease. Lots of healing takes place when you sleep as your body detoxifies and focuses its attention on cleansing and restoration. When you sleep, your body regenerates itself. You body repairs blood and brain cells and regenerates muscles and even your skin. A good night's rest can go farther than an expensive skin cream to renewing your face's healthy glow. Rest is also noted to make you smarter—or at least allow your intelligence to shine when you're taking a test.

Like the two leaders of the wagon train discovered, taking time to rest can actually lead to greater efficiency, productivity, and speed. The idea may seem counterintuitive, but rest can actually enable you to go farther and get more done.

Rest also does something powerful within our souls. When we stop, we are in a better position to allow God to move in our lives. Rest is a physical reminder that we are not in control of everything and, at the end of the day we are not the ones who have to hold it all together. That is God's job. Rest reminds us of our place, not just in life, but in Him.

Indeed, the benefits of rest are greater than we can possibly imagine.

1. Have you ever had an experience like the leader of the wagon train where rest actually helped you get more done? If so, describe.

2. To what unhealthy alternatives are you tempted to turn when you're not well rested?

3. What benefits do you notice in your own life when you're well rested?

One of the many things that rob you of rest is worry. When you worry, it's difficult—if not impossible—for you to enjoy the peace and rest that God has for you.

*4. Read **Matthew 6:25–32**. What things should you not worry about according to this passage?*

Though we are not to worry about these kinds of things, they are still a part of our lives. We still need sustenance and clothing and basic provisions in order to survive. Yet these are not to become the center of life, because if they do, they can rob us of rest and distract us from what's truly important.

5. Read *Matthew 6:33–34. According to this passage what is truly important? How does worry rob you of the rest God wants to give you?*

Often our attitudes affect our outlook on life. The way we look at life affects the way we live life.

6. Read **Psalm 131**. *How would you describe the attitude of the psalmist in verse 1? How does this result in rest for the soul of the psalmist?*

7. What choice does the psalmist make in **Psalm 131:2** regarding rest?

8. What does it mean to you to "still and quiet" your soul? How does having a "still and quiet" soul help better prepare you for the challenges you face every day?

The truth is that rest restores and renews our bodies, minds, and spirits. Rest is a physical reminder that we are not in control of everything and at the end of the day, we are not the ones who have to hold it all together. That is God's job.

Digging Deeper

When we seek and obey God, we find rest for our souls. Read **Isaiah 32:17**. Why do you think the fruit of the righteous is peace? How does living righteously—obeying God's laws—lead to quietness and confidence? Is it possible to be at peace and truly rest when you're knowingly disobeying God? Why or why not?

Ponder and Pray

The opening Scripture for this lesson comes from **Isaiah 28:12**, "To whom he said, 'This is the resting place, let the weary rest'; and, 'This is the place of repose'—but they would not listen." At what points in life are you most tempted to turn down an opportunity to rest? Are there any correlations between the times you turn down an opportunity to rest and the times you need it most? What changes do you need to make to be able to enter the resting place God has for you?

Bonus Activity

Over the course of the next week, let yourself take a nap at least one afternoon. Even if you don't fall asleep, take at least fifteen to twenty minutes to close your eyes, pray, and relax. Share how the experience affected your interaction with someone else.

Three

Know Your Season

He shall be like a tree
Planted by the rivers of water,
That brings forth its fruit in its season,
Whose leaf also shall not wither;
And whatever he does shall prosper.

—PSALM 1:3, NKJV

What is your favorite season? Do you enjoy the new budding life and beauty of spring? Do you prefer the long, hot days of summer? Do you love the wonder of a crisp, colorful fall? Or do you prefer the cold, still days of winter?

Every season is distinct. Spring marks new life. Summer displays steady growth. Fall is the season of busy harvest. Winter is a time of retreat and rest before the cycle of seasons begins again. Depending on where you live, the seasons may be subtly or significantly different from each other. But have you ever taken time to think about the seasons in your own life? Sometimes the speed of your life is connected to the season in your life.

There are seasons of busyness before big projects are due. There are seasons of transition when a move is in progress. There are seasons of celebration when a marriage is performed, a new life is born, a milestone in life is achieved. There are seasons of rest when you take time to retreat, vacation, or get away.

Just as every season in our world has its own distinct beauty, every season in life does, too! Some seasons are naturally longer than others. You may be in a season of being single, a newlywed, a parent, grandparent, or even great-grandparent. You may be in a season of immediate deadlines or a slower season when you can catch your breath. Whether you're juggling a dozen balls or only one, it's important to not only recognize but celebrate the season you're in!

If you're in a spring season, you may be experiencing new life in your relationships, your workplace, or even your family. There's probably a sense of excitement and even a little uncertainty with all the new things "budding" in your life. Spring can be an incredibly enjoyable season, particularly after a long, hard winter.

If you're in a summer season, you're probably working hard and enjoying the life that comes with long days. If you look closely, you'll probably recognize healthy growth in your life. The heat may be a little (or a lot) uncomfortable, and on some days, you may be tempted to begin counting down the days until fall.

If you're in a fall season, you're probably enjoying the harvest of hard work. Things you have waited, hoped, and prayed for are finally happening. The fruit of your labor is sweet. Now that doesn't mean the work is over—in fact, you may be busier than ever—but there's a sense that all that you've been doing is being rewarded.

If you're in a winter season, you may feel a little disconnected without the sense of new life and productivity of the other seasons. Winters can be long and hard. But never doubt that God is doing things deep within you, and before you know it, spring will be right around the corner.

The truth is that in every season of life God does things within us that can't be done in any other season. Whether springing to a new career or stage in life, growing right where we are, enjoying the harvest of our work, or laying fallow, God is present and at work in our lives. No matter what season we're in, there's something to celebrate when it comes to what God is doing in us.

1. *When you think about the seasons—spring, summer, fall, or winter—which is your favorite? Why?*

2. *When you think about the seasons in terms of your life— spring, summer, fall, or winter—which is your favorite? Least favorite? Why?*

3. *What season—spring, summer, fall, or winter—would you say you're in right now in your life? What do you like about this season? What do you dislike?*

The book of Ecclesiastes reveals that there is a time and season for everything under heaven.

4. Read **Ecclesiastes 3:1–8**. *In the following space, fill in each of the pairs listed in each verse. Then, circle the word you naturally prefer in each pair.*

Example:

Ecclesiastes 3:2 ___(born)___ *and*_____ *die* _____.

Ecclesiastes 3:2 _____ *and*_____.

Ecclesiastes 3:3 _____ *and*_____.

Ecclesiastes 3:3 _____ *and*_____.

Ecclesiastes 3:4 _____ *and*_____.

Ecclesiastes 3:4 _____ *and*_____.

Ecclesiastes 3:5 _____ *and*_____.

Ecclesiastes 3:5 _____ *and*_____.

Ecclesiastes 3:6 _____ *and*_____.

Ecclesiastes 3:6 _____ *and*_____.

Ecclesiastes 3:7 _____ *and*_____.

Ecclesiastes 3:7 _____ *and*_____.

Ecclesiastes 3:8 _____ *and*_____.

Ecclesiastes 3:8 _____ *and*_____.

5. *Why do you think you naturally prefer some seasons over others? Are there any seasons in which God cannot work or redeem?*

6. *How does recognizing the season you're in allow you to trust and rest in what God is doing in your life?*

No matter what season you're in, God desires for you to find rest.

7. *Read Exodus 34:21. Why do you think the verse says, "Even during the plowing season and harvest you must rest"?*

8. *What are the "seasons" in life when you're tempted to overwork and skip rest? Even in your busiest seasons, why is it important to make time to rest?*

The truth is that in every season of life—including our spiritual life—God does things within us that can't be done in any other season. No matter what season you're in, there's something to celebrate when it comes to what God is doing in you.

Digging Deeper

Since the beginning, God has established seasons for the earth. Read **Genesis 8:22**. Why do you think God designed nature to constantly be changing from season to season? What does this reveal about God's desire to do something new in you?

Ponder and Pray

The opening Scripture for this lesson comes from **Psalm 1:3**, "He shall be like a tree planted by the rivers of water, that brings forth its fruit in its season, whose leaf also shall not wither; and whatever he does shall prosper" (NKJV). At what moments in your life have you felt as if this verse described you? What does it personally mean for you to be "planted by rivers of water"? Why is this so important for yielding fruit in its season?

Bonus Activity

Now that you've taken an inventory of the season that you're in, go ahead and celebrate it. Look at the calendar: what physical season are you in? How can you make the most of it?

Go to the beach. Head out for a hike. Make jam or jelly. Plant flowers. Enjoy an afternoon of cocoa with a friend. Throw a harvest party. Then think about your spiritual season. How can you make the most of it, as well?

Spend an afternoon in prayer and worship. Take a Saturday to volunteer at a local organization. Plan a family outreach adventure. Support a new charity. Write an encouraging note to someone who needs it. Whatever season you're in, do something to celebrate it!

Applying the Breaks

As you begin to discover the importance of rest even in a busy schedule, you'll notice that from time to time you need to embrace the breaks in order to apply the brakes. Learning to slow down, say "no," and rest isn't always easy, but, as you'll discover in the next few chapters, it's essential to discovering the rest God has for you.

Four

The Gift of Sabbath

*By the seventh day God had finished the work he
had been doing; so on the seventh day he rested
from all his work.*

—GENESIS 2:2

When was the last time you rested? *Really* rested? In our fast-paced, multitasking world, the idea of resting—let alone taking a day of rest each week—seems foreign, almost mythical, in a world that is addicted to hurry.

Real rest demands that we stop completely. We stop the frantic pace. We stop checking things off our to-do list. We stop measuring our worth by our productivity.

And that's not always easy. Performing is often easier than simply being. If you go too long without rest, it can feel foreign—you don't quite know what to do with yourself. Maybe that's one reason God commands that we rest regularly.

During Creation, God demonstrated this kind of rest. After six days of creating and designing, He took a full day to rest. God didn't need to rest because He was not physically tired. God rested as a demonstration to all of creation of the need for rest. In fact, of the Ten Commandments, one whole commandment is dedicated toward keeping the Sabbath—a weekly reminder that we all need physical rest.

The idea of taking Sabbath or finding time to rest is an invitation to rest and renew yourself. The Sabbath asks us to take a break from a busy schedule and never-ending "to-do" list and take one day to rest our souls, reorder our worlds, and realign ourselves with God.

In fact, God didn't just establish a Sabbath day, but also a Sabbath year as described in Leviticus 25. Every seventh year the land lays fallow, which allows the soil to recover. The Sabbath year is an agricultural mirror of the Sabbath day, both of which teach us an important lesson in trusting God. When we avoid doing work—including little things like laundry, cleaning, or cooking—then we demonstrate our trust in God and His provision for our lives.

Our culture often tells us that time is money. The Sabbath reminds us that time is holy. A day off reminds us that we belong to God—our Creator, our Provider, and the Source of our strength. As you embrace the Sabbath in your own life, remember to be kind and grace-giving to yourself. Expect things to not go according to your plans. And always look for the joy. The Sabbath is a gift. Are you ready to receive it?

1. Have you ever gone so long without rest that when you did try to rest you didn't know what to do with yourself? If so, explain.

2. Why do you think God established the pattern of Sabbath—or taking one day off a week—from the beginning of time?

3. What advice do you have for someone who can't take off the same day every week or even a full day because of their work schedule?

In the Old Testament, the idea of Sabbath is introduced after God's people had been in slavery and captivity. The Sabbath was designed by God to give the people rest and allow them to stop working and reconnect with Him.

4. Read **Exodus 20:8–11**. What does it mean to you to keep the Sabbath "holy"?

5. *Why do you think the passage instructs that everyone in the household—including the animals—should rest? In what ways can rest be contagious?*

Throughout His earthly ministry, Jesus was often criticized for His activities—particularly healing people—on the Sabbath. While Jesus knew it was important to honor the Sabbath, He recognized that there were some things that were more important.

6. *Read **Mark 2:23–27**. What do you think Jesus meant when He said, "The Sabbath was made for man, not man for the Sabbath"?*

7. *Do you tend to view the idea of Sabbath as more of a burden or a gift? Explain.*

8. *In what ways have you set apart a Sabbath or a day of rest in your schedule? How has it affected you, your relationships, or your life?*

Digging Deeper

The Sabbath wasn't just something for the Israelites. The Book of Hebrews reminds us that the teaching and principle behind the Sabbath extends to all people for all time. Read **Hebrews 4:9–11**. Why is the idea of Sabbath rest so important for your spiritual life? How does taking time to unplug give you the opportunity to plug back into a closer relationship with God?

> *The truth is that the Sabbath is a gift from God. The Sabbath reminds us that time is holy. The Sabbath asks us to put the breaks on a busy schedule and take time to rest our souls, reorder our worlds, and realign ourselves with God.*

Ponder and Pray

The opening Scripture for this lesson comes from **Genesis 2:2**, "By the seventh day God had finished the work he had been doing; so on the seventh day he rested from all his work." Does anything ever stop you from "finishing the work" you've been doing? Why do you think recognizing finishing lines is important in daily life?

Bonus Activity

Select one day this week to celebrate the Sabbath. Go ahead and decide ahead of time what you will and will not do in order to make the day special. As you approach the day, try not to be legalistic. If you determine not to use your cell phone on the Sabbath, and then you get a flat tire, of course you should use your cell phone! At the end of the day, observe how the scheduled downtime affected your relationship with God.

Five

The Power of Margins

The LORD is good to those whose hope is in him,
to the one who seeks him.

—LAMENTATIONS 3:25

Imagine a glass placed in front of you. Now imagine taking a pitcher of water and filling the glass. The glass has a natural limit. If you keep pouring beyond that limit, the water will overflow onto the table and eventually the floor.

In the same way, each of us has a natural limit on how much we can contain, do, and manage well. When we go beyond our natural limits, the overflow is not necessarily healthy. We may overflow in the form of stress, anxiety, anger, disappointment, or even depression.

Despite this simple principle, many of us are tempted to live our lives as if we had no limits, as if we could pour all day long without over-flow. Our schedules have no wiggle room. Our lives have no space for error or interruptions or even the unexpected. One more drop and we're pushed over the edge. Time to rest, recuperate, and reconnect with God evaporates. And we find ourselves maxed out physically, emotionally, and spiritually.

The good news is that you don't have to overfill your glass. You can be proactive about embracing a healthy-paced lifestyle that has margins. You can get the max out of life without maxing out your life. It all begins with establishing margins.

Now imagine another glass placed in front of you. Imagine taking a pitcher of water and filling the glass, but this time you stop half an inch from the rim. There's room for more. There's space for the occasional overflow. So when the unexpected things of life come along—a surprise deadline, a last-minute call from a friend in town, an unexpected expense—you're better prepared to handle it.

Margins are incredibly powerful. When we build margins into our lives, we give more opportunities for God to be at work in our lives and in the lives of those around us.

1. *Imagine a glass filled with water. Do you tend to live your life as if the glass was mostly filled, completely filled, or overflowing?*

2. *Why do you think margins are so important in your life—both physical and spiritual? Why do you think people are tempted to live life without them?*

3. In what areas of life are you least likely to leave margins: your finances, your schedule, your health, some other area?

Psalm 23 offers a beautiful portrait of God as our Shepherd.

4. Read **Psalm 23:1–3**. As a Good Shepherd, what does God do for His sheep in these verses?

5. In what ways have you experienced the things listed in **Psalm 23:1–3**?

6. Do you think it's possible to be too busy to enjoy the green pastures and quiet waters God has for you? Why or why not?

The truth is that when we build margins into our lives, then we give more opportunities for God to be at work within us as well as in the lives of those around us.

7. In what ways does having margins enable you to enjoy all God has for you?

8. What changes do you need to make in your life right now in order to have healthier margins?

Digging Deeper

Without margins, it's easy for stress to get the best of us. We can even find ourselves upset or angry over small issues. Read **James 1:19–20**. How does having margins in your life make it easier to obey the instructions found in this verse? How does having margins help you to be more patient and kind?

Ponder and Pray

The opening Scripture for this lesson comes from **Lamentations 3:25**, "The Lord is good to those whose hope is in him, to the one who seeks him." In what ways have you built margins into your current schedule to seek God? In what ways have you experienced the goodness of the Lord in the last week?

Bonus Activity

Take a moment and reflect on your schedule for the upcoming week. Intentionally schedule in at least one afternoon and two evenings to simply relax at home. At the end of the week, note how the scheduled downtime affected your attitude and relationships as well as your relationship with God.

Six

The Fine Art of Saying "No"

It is vain for you to rise up early,
To sit up late,
To eat the bread of sorrows;
For so He gives His beloved sleep.

—PSALM 127:2, NKJV

"No." It's one of the smallest, simplest, and easiest to pronounce words. Many mothers will list it among the most popular and emphatic words that their two-year-olds learn to say. Yet as we grow older, "no" can become more and more difficult to say.

Many of us are naturally wired to want to please and try to meet the expectations of others. We may be tempted to say "yes" to something we really don't want to do because a little voice inside us whispers, "I will disappoint her if I don't do this," "I will cause conflict if I don't give in," and "It's just easier to say yes than no."

Saying "no" isn't easy. Some of us fear failure. Others fear disappointing those they love. Some fall into the trap of feeling like they have to save everyone and everything. Others are tempted to be people-pleasers. And most of us feel guilty for saying "no" at one time or another. Yet when you avoid saying "no," it's harder to establish healthy boundaries for yourself, your family, and your schedule. If you're not careful, resentment can creep into your life and you can end up feeling used or taken advantage of. When you do too much, the result can be burnout, exhaustion, and lack of motivation.

Fortunately, God has provided a way to avoid overcommitting yourself. And it begins with prayer. When you take time to pray and commit each day to the Lord, asking for His wisdom in your activities, a transformation takes place in your life. Instead of simply reacting to an opportunity or need, you can proactively seek God's will and wisdom. The result is a more healthfully paced and effective life.

How do you learn to practice the fine art of saying "no"? Primarily by saying "yes" to God first! At the beginning of each day, take time to pray and ask God to order your steps. Ask Him to bring the people and opportunities into your life that He has for you. As different opportunities come up, resist the urge to give a knee-jerk response. Instead, develop a habit of asking for time to think about it, look at your schedule, and most importantly, pray. If you know right away that something isn't right for you, a simple but direct, "I can't help you with that" or "I'm already overcommitted" is the best answer.

Though saying "no" can be very difficult, it's also one of the healthiest things you can learn to do. When you learn to say "no," you open up the door to say "yes" to other things—including rest and healthy boundaries.

1. In what kind of situations and to what kinds of requests is it hardest for you to say "no"? Why do you think it's so difficult to say "no" at these times and to these things?

2. When was the last time you were caught in a situation where you struggled to say "no"? How did you handle the situation?

3. Have you developed a graceful response for saying "no" when you're asked to get involved or commit to something you simply can't do? If so, what is it?

King David was known as a man after God's own heart. As king, it was crucial for David to know when to say "yes" and when to say "no" in certain situations.

4. Read **1 Chronicles 14:8–10**. David could have responded with an instant response to the situation with the Philistines, but he decided to inquire of God first. Why do you think taking time to inquire of God is so important in our daily lives?

5. Have you ever inquired of God regarding a particular situation or opportunity and felt as if the response was "yes," "no," or "go"? If so, describe. How did taking time to pray before you decided better enable you to handle the situation?

The truth is that while saying "no" can be difficult, it's one of the best things you can learn to do. When you learn to say "no," you open up the door to say "yes" to other things—including rest, healthy boundaries, and a more balanced life.

6. Read 1 Chronicles 14:11–17. In this passage, David inquires of God again. How does God's response differ in verses 14–15 compared to verse 10?

7. What does this passage reveal about the importance of inquiring of God?

8. Are there any opportunities or areas of your life in which you need to talk to God about your involvement? Are there any opportunities that you need to say "yes" to or graciously decline?

Digging Deeper

Inquiring of God is not a one-time event, but an ongoing process. Read **1 Samuel 23:1–14.** In this passage, David's inquiring of God helped preserve his life as well as the lives of his soldiers. How does inquiring of God help build a stronger relationship with God? How does inquiring of God help you grow in your faith?

Ponder and Pray

The opening Scripture for this lesson comes from **Psalm 127:2**, "It is vain for you to rise up early, to sit up late, to eat the bread of sorrows; for so He gives His beloved sleep" (NKJV). Are you ever tempted to pack too many things into your day? How does it make you feel? Why do you think the verse says, "He gives His beloved sleep"? In what ways is sleep a gift from God?

Bonus Activity

Make a list of several different gracious responses that you can give someone on-the-spot when you're asked to do something. Practice saying them out loud. Over the course of the next week, look for an opportunity to use your ready-made response when asked to get involved in something new. Then spend time thinking and praying about whether it's something God is inviting you to get involved in. Record your progress as you get better at discerning God's responses regarding your agenda.

Rest as a Lifestyle

Have you ever thought about making rest a part of your lifestyle? Not just a scheduled break, but a part of your very existence? Rest can be a regular part of your life as you prayerfully seek ways to incorporate it into your everyday existence. The next few chapters highlight the importance of having rest be an intrinsic part of the way you live, and how you can practically apply it in your own life.

Seven

Your Home, Your Sanctuary

Unless the LORD builds the house,
its builders labor in vain.

—PSALM 127:1

Have you ever stopped to think about all the work that went into building the place where you live? The architects. The builders. The construction crew. The designers—not just of the building but of everything it contains! Someone developed your flooring, someone built your walls, and someone designed the chair you sit on when you eat. A lot of work went into the design of your home.

Just as careful thought and care goes into building a house, a lot of thought and care is required to transform a place of residence into a home and, more importantly, a sanctuary for you and your family.

How would you describe the atmosphere of your home? Is it a place of chaos or beauty? A place of strife or peace? A place of restlessness or renewal? A peaceful, restful atmosphere isn't based on the number of people in your home or even the neatness, but the attitudes of the people in your home. Your home can be a sanctuary, a place of rest and renewal, not just for your soul, but for those who visit as well.

The apostle Paul demonstrated this beautifully in **Acts 28**. He went to Rome to share the good news of Jesus and decided to stay. **Acts 28:30–31** says, "For two whole years Paul stayed there in his own rented house and welcomed all who came to see him. Boldly and without hindrance he preached the kingdom of God and taught about the Lord Jesus Christ."

This passage is a reminder that it doesn't matter whether you own your home or whether you rent, if you've lived there your whole life or only a few short years. And it doesn't matter how big or small your house might be. Paul's secret in transforming his temporary house into a home was that he welcomed all who came to see him. He used his home as a place to connect with others and share the good news of Jesus.

No matter how small or large, you can design your home as a place that welcomes rest and renewal and invites people to connect with God. Simple things like asking God to use your home to bless others, selecting a sacred space to study and pray, or developing a library of resources that can help you grow in your faith can go a long way toward helping your home become a sanctuary. As you commit your life and home to Him, you'll be surprised how quickly God begins to use you and your home as a source of refreshment for others.

1. What is the kindest, most meaningful thing that a visitor has said about your home?

2. How would you describe the atmosphere of your home?

3. In what ways is your home like a sanctuary to you?

4. Read **Joshua 24:15**. In what ways can a home be a reflection of your spiritual life?

5. *How can your home be a place that encourages you and others to pursue a relationship with God?*

Your home is a place where you can naturally express generosity, kindness, and hospitality to others. You can use your home to refresh the souls of others even as your own soul is refreshed.

6. *Read 1 Peter 4:9–10. Why do you think a good attitude is so important when it comes to being hospitable? Is it possible to be hospitable without a good attitude? Why or why not?*

It's easy sometimes to look around your home and be distracted by what you don't have or what you're missing. Things like clutter, cat hair, out-of-date furniture, or even a tight budget can make us think we aren't the best candidates to offer hospitality. But the Bible makes it clear that everyone should practice hospitality.

7. Read **Romans 12:9–13**. Make a list of the things instructed in this passage in the space provided. How does each of those things create rest for you? For others?

8. If people who visited your home could experience just one thing, what would you want them to say about your home?

> *The truth is that your home can be a sanctuary, a place of rest and renewal not just for your soul, but for those who visit as well.*

Digging Deeper

In ancient times, hospitality was essential for safe, successful travel. Early believers needed other believers to open up their homes if they were to have a safe place to stay. Read **3 John 5–6**. Why do you think it's so important to use your home as a place to bless and encourage others? Do you think that offering your home as a sanctuary for others is as important today as it was in ancient times? Why or why not?

Ponder and Pray

The opening Scripture for this lesson comes from **Psalm 127:1**, "Unless the LORD builds the house, its builders labor in vain." Do you tend to think of your house as your own house or God's house? When was the last time you asked God to use your home to bless and encourage others? What was the outcome?

Bonus Activity

Think of someone within your neighborhood, church, or community whose home is like a sanctuary for you. Take time to write a letter to the person who owns the home to let them know. Thank the person not just for their hospitality and kindness, but also for the way they allow their home to be a place of rest and restoration.

Eight

Discovering the Secret Place

He who dwells in the shelter of the Most High
will rest in the shadow of the Almighty.

—PSALM 91:1

Brother Lawrence was a monk in the seventeenth century who is known for his close relationship with God as described in the classic Christian book *The Practice of the Presence of God*. As a monk, Brother Lawrence spent most of his life working in the kitchen and repairing shoes in his later years. No matter how mundane or repetitive his work, he found great joy and comfort in his relationship with God. He discovered that even the simplest of activities—from washing dishes to frying food—can become acts of worship if a person's heart is focused on honoring God. Brother Lawrence lived as if there was no one else but God and him in the world—and that commitment changed him from the inside out. Those around him couldn't help but notice an unmistakable sense of peace that accompanied Brother Lawrence wherever he went.

Brother Lawrence discovered a profound peace and rest in God's presence. He discovered what is sometimes referred to as the "secret place" in Scripture. **Psalm 91:1** says, "He who dwells in the shelter of the Most High will rest in the shadow of the Almighty." The King James Version of the Bible translates "shelter" as "secret place," and the original Hebrew word means "covering" or "hiding place." Thus, **Psalm 91:1** is a reminder that when we abide in God, He becomes our covering, our hiding place, and our refuge. That doesn't mean that difficult things won't happen, but that when they do we can still be at rest because we are hiding in Him.

Like Brother Lawrence, people around us won't be able to help but notice an unmistakable sense of peace within us when we are abiding in Him.

1. *Brother Lawrence discovered that the simplest of activities could become acts of worship if you focus your attention on God. Have you ever had a Brother Lawrence-type experience where you found yourself worshiping God while washing the dishes, cleaning the house, or doing something mundane? If so, describe.*

2. *Do you think God wants to be involved in your life even in the mundane or especially in the mundane? Explain.*

3. When in your life has God been a "secret place" or "hiding place" for you? What did you discover about yourself and God through that experience?

Everyone has a unique way of describing their desire for God. The book of Psalms offers many expressions of desiring God and a closer relationship with Him.

*4. Read **Psalm 84:2**. In the space that follows and in your own words, describe your own desire to know God and abide in Him.*

The secret place or hiding place of God provides a peace that the world can't offer.

5. Read **John 14:27**. How have you found this verse to be true? If possible, describe a moment in your life when you experienced this kind of peace.

6. Read **John 15:1–8**. According to this passage, why is it so important to abide in God and make Him your refuge?

7. At what times in your life is it most difficult to abide in Christ and find your secret place in Him? At what times in your life is it easiest to abide in Christ and find your secret place in Him?

8. *What does it mean to you to abide in God? What changes do you need to make in your life to make God your abiding place?*

Digging Deeper

The secret place is also a place of prayer and connecting with God. Read **Matthew 6:5–6**. Where do you go to get away from everything and pray? How does prayer help you to abide in God? How does it change you?

The truth is that God desires for you to abide in Him and discover Him as your refuge. When you abide in the secret place of God, you can't help but discover rest for your soul.

Ponder and Pray

The opening Scripture for this lesson comes from **Psalm 91:9**, "He who dwells in the shelter of the Most High will rest in the shadow of the Almighty." Read **Psalm 91:2**. Identify a time in your life when God was your fortress. How did God guard and protect you? How did it affect your faith in Him?

Bonus Activity

Try practicing the presence of God this week. In your daily activities, particularly the most mundane, intentionally choose to spend time in prayer and worship. Ask God to focus your thoughts and heart on Him. Note how it changes your attitudes and affections.

Nine

Moments of Retreat

"Come with me by yourselves to a quiet place and get some rest."

—MARK 6:31

Why are moments of retreat so important? Because sometimes you have to retreat in order to advance. Retreats, times when you get away from the busy demands of everyday life, allow you to recharge physically, emotionally, and spiritually.

In the presence of unhurried quietness, you can take time to decelerate and slow down. You can catch your breath and allow your body the rest that it needs. You can sleep in and allow yourself to do nothing more than enjoy curling up on a couch or sitting outside under the warm sun and cool breeze. Moments of retreat rejuvenate the body.

Those moments also rejuvenate the soul. When you get away, you are given the opportunity to regain perspective on life. You can ask yourself, *How am I really doing?* and take time to think and pray about the answer. Getting away allows for healthy introspection—the kind that helps you discern where to spend your energy and where you should be cutting back.

Moments of retreat also restore the spirit. They provide an opportunity to really slow down and reconnect with God through prayer, study, and worship. Retreats can allow time to practice spiritual disciplines such as silence or fasting. They provide time to recognize God for who He is as well as His presence in your life, and to adore Him with an undistracted heart.

Retreat allows us to savor life, embrace God, and enjoy rest. While a weekend or weeklong retreat is something to try to do on a regular basis, it's also important to recognize the shorter, more accessible moments of retreat in life. An early morning of undistracted prayer. An afternoon of rest and rejuvenation. A late-night time of personal study and reflection. These kinds of mini-retreats can provide much-needed opportunities to get away and unplug. You just might be surprised how much a little retreat helps you advance in your life, your relationships, and your faith.

1. *When was the last time you went on a spiritual retreat that lasted more than a day? Where did you go? What was most meaningful to you about the experience?*

2. *Have you ever taken a mini-retreat to get away and reconnect with God? If so, what did you do? What was most meaningful to you about the experience?*

3. Why do you think it's so important to take moments to retreat from the busyness of life?

4. Read **Psalm 46:10**. On a scale of 1 to 10, how difficult is it to follow the instructions in this verse? Why do you think it can be difficult?

During moments of retreat, we are invited to rest and prayerfully seek God. Sometimes it's difficult to decelerate from the busyness of life to a restful retreat. You may find it difficult to be still or to be surrounded by so much silence.

5. During moments of retreat, do you tend to struggle more with stillness or silence? Explain.

Throughout His earthly ministry, Jesus repeatedly withdrew from the busyness of ministry to get away.

> 6. *On the chart, match the Scripture to the place where Jesus went to find a moment of retreat.*

Bible Passage	Where Jesus went to retreat
Matthew 14:13	He withdrew to a lonely place such as the wilderness.
Matthew 15:21	The Spirit led Him into the desert.
Mark 3:7	He withdrew by boat to a solitary place.
Luke 5:16	He withdrew to the region of Tyre and Sidon.
Mark 1:12	He withdrew with His disciples to a lake.

> 7. *Reflecting on the chart above, why do you think Jesus took moments of retreat so often? Do you see any pattern in the places, method, or style of retreat that He took? If so, explain. If not, explain.*

8. *Reflecting on the chart above, read* **Luke 5:16**. *What activity did Jesus do during His moments of retreat? Why is this activity so important to incorporate into your own personal times of retreat?*

Digging Deeper

Moments of retreat are important for our physical, emotional, and spiritual health. Read **Ecclesiastes 4:6**. In what ways do you find this verse to be true in your own life? How does taking time to get away help give you a better perspective on your work?

The truth is that sometimes you have to retreat in order to advance. Retreats—times when you get away from the busy demands of everyday life—allow you to recharge physically, emotionally, and spiritually

Ponder and Pray

The opening Scripture for this lesson comes from **Mark 6:31**, "Come with me by yourselves to a quiet place and get some rest." Spend some time praying through the words of this verse. What is the most challenging part of the verse for you?

Bonus Activity

Schedule a moment of retreat during the upcoming week. Spend a morning, afternoon, or evening getting away to rest and refocus on your relationship with God. Turn off the cell phone and the computer. Find a place where you can get away and be still.

Resting in God

Learning to rest in God means resting not only in who God is, but in what He has done and what He will do. As you deepen your relationship with God, you can't help but discover rest for your soul.

Ten

Resting in Who He Is

Submit to God and be at peace with him;
in this way prosperity will come to you.

—JOB 22:21

What is the most valuable thing that you've ever lost? How did you become aware that it was gone? All of us have lost things of value from time to time during the course of our lives. But one of the most valuable things you can lose without even realizing it is a healthy perspective!

The good news is that God makes it possible for you to keep a healthy perspective at all times by hiding His Word in your heart. He invites you to study the Scriptures and get to know Him. He invites you to see how women and men have lived faith-filled lives in centuries past so you can live a God-honoring life today.

In the Scriptures, you discover who God is and what He's done. You begin to see His incredible love and desire for a personal relationship with you. Throughout the Bible, you find that God has given commands and instructions that help you live the best life possible. As you seek Him above all else, you find yourself discovering peace and rest like none other you've experienced.

So how do you hide God's Word in your heart? Through reading, studying, and memorizing Scripture. As you tuck verses and passages away in your heart and mind, the Holy Spirit can bring them to your mind as you need them. Scriptures can be a source of comfort, correction, guidance, and peace.

Colossians 3:16 instructs, "Let the peace of Christ dwell in you richly as you teach and admonish one another with all wisdom, and as you sing psalms, hymns and spiritual songs with gratitude in your hearts to God."

As you hide God's Word in your heart, you'll not only find yourself strengthened, but you'll find yourself strengthening and encouraging others. Hiding God's Word in your heart helps you to know God even better! And as you know God, you discover Him as your Source of joy, strength, peace, and rest.

1. Have you ever memorized any Scriptures before? If so, how did it affect your faith? Your attitude?

2. Why do you think getting to know the Scriptures is so important?

3. *Have you ever been in a certain situation where a Scripture helped provide the guidance, strength, or peace that you needed? How can knowing and studying the Scriptures be a source of rest for your soul?*

4. *Read the following Scriptures. How does each one help you to increase your ability to obey God and rest in Him?*

   Psalm 19:8:

   Psalm 103:1:

   Psalm 119:11:

   Psalm 119:40:

*5. Read **Hebrews 4:12**. Describe a moment in your own life when you found this verse to be true.*

God is recognized by different names throughout the Scriptures. These names offer insights into His character and who God really is.

6. On the following chart, fill in the meaning of the name of God to match the name and Scripture reference.

Name of God	Scripture Reference	Meaning of Name of God
Yahweh Jireh (Yireh)	Genesis 22:14	
Yahweh Nissi	Exodus 17:15	
Yahweh Shalom	Judges 6:24	
Yahweh Sabbaoth	1 Samuel 1:3	
Yahweh Ro'i	Psalm 23:1	
Yahweh Elohim Israel	Isaiah 17:6	
Yahweh Tsidkenu	Jeremiah 23:6	

7. How does knowing the meanings of the names of God impact your faith?

8. What steps do you need to take to get to know God even better?

The truth is that hiding God's Word in your heart helps you to know God even better! And as you know God, you discover Him as your source of joy, strength, peace, and rest.

Digging Deeper

Studying the Scripture isn't just getting to know a book—it's getting to know God. Read **John 5:39**. Why do you think Jesus made this observation? When are you most tempted to forget that studying the Bible is really an invitation to know God better?

Ponder and Pray

The opening Scripture for this lesson comes from **Job 22:21**, "Submit to God and be at peace with him; in this way prosperity will come to you." How does submitting to God affect the level of peace and rest in your life? In what ways have you been blessed by following God's commands and instructions?

Bonus Activity

During the upcoming week, select at least two verses from this study and commit them to memory. You may choose to write them down on note cards and place them around the house or even record them on your cell phone and play them back throughout the week.

Eleven

Resting in What He's Done

How great is the love the Father has lavished on us,
that we should be called children of God!
And that is what we are!

—1 JOHN 3:1

There's an often-told proverbial story about a famous tightrope walker who visited Niagara Falls. He decided to stretch his rope across the steep waterfall. In front of nerve-racked crowds, he walked and eventually picked up enough speed to run across the falls. Then, he did it a second time blindfolded. Still wearing the blindfold, he agreed to make the journey a third time. This time he pushed a wheelbarrow. He successfully made it across, and the crowds shouted and applauded in amazement.

The famous tightrope walker shouted, "Who believes I can push a man in this wheelbarrow across the falls?"

A young man in the front row waved his hands and yelled, "I do! I believe!"

"Then come climb in the wheelbarrow," replied the tightrope walker.

The story is a wonderful illustration of the journey of faith. Throughout the Bible, we read of men and women who survived perilous journeys. In faith, Abraham left his homeland for a new land even though he did not know where he was going. Sarah became pregnant long after the age of her fertility had passed. As an infant Moses survived an edict that Israelite babies should be killed. Daniel miraculously survived the lions' den. The Bible is filled with men and women who climbed into the wheelbarrow of faith and trusted God with everything they had.

Throughout the Bible we also discover what God has done for us. We discover a God who answers prayers, who calls us by name, who cleanses of us sin, and who comforts, corrects, and counsels us. We discover a God who knows us, who leads us, who listens to us. We discover a God who saves, sustains, and strengthens. We discover a God who never sleeps or slumbers, but always has us on His mind.

When you know God and what He's done, it's easier to step into the wheelbarrow and rest in Him, no matter what perilous journey you might be facing.

1. Why do you think it can be difficult to climb into the wheelbarrow of faith and trust God with everything?

2. *Have you ever stepped into the wheelbarrow before? Have you ever been tempted to step back out? Explain.*

3. *Why is knowing what God has done so important in strengthening your faith and resting in Him?*

4. *What attributes or characteristics of God are mentioned in the following verses?*

Numbers 23:19:

Deuteronomy 4:31:

Deuteronomy 7:9:

2 Peter 3:9:

5. *How do the attributes mentioned in the verses above strengthen your faith? Do they make you more likely or less likely to want to step into the wheelbarrow? Explain.*

One of God's characteristics is His faithfulness. He is faithful even when we are faithless.

> 6. Look up the following Scriptures. How does each one make you want to trust God and rest in His promises even more?

> *Psalm 119:89–90:*

> *Isaiah 46:11:*

> *Isaiah 54:10:*

> 7. Have you ever felt as if God has dropped you out of the wheelbarrow? Explain.

8. In what ways is God asking you to trust Him and rest in Him even more right now?

The truth is that when you know God and what He has done, it's easier to step into the wheelbarrow and rest in Him no matter what journey you might be facing.

Digging Deeper

Sometimes it can be hard to have faith, yet God invites us to trust Him. Read **Hebrews 11:1**. How would you define *faith* in your own words? In your own life? If you wanted to explain faith to someone, how would you describe it?

Ponder and Pray

The opening Scripture for this lesson comes from **1 John 3:1**, "How great is the love the Father has lavished on us, that we should be called children of God! And that is what we are!" In what ways do you see yourself as a child of God? Does anything prevent you from seeing yourself as God's child? Do you think there's anything you can do to lose God as your Father?

Bonus Activity

During the upcoming week spend some time reading through old journals, diaries, or letters. Take note of God's faithfulness in your life—those moments when He has revealed Himself to you. How does knowing that God has been faithful in the past help you know He will be faithful in the future?

Twelve

Resting in What He Will Do

Yes, I am coming soon.

—REVELATION 22:20

In *Putting the One Minute Manager to Work*, Kenneth Blanchard and Robert Lorber tell the story of a man who went hiking alone one day. As he climbed the mountain, he slipped and fell off a cliff. He managed to miraculously grab a branch on his way down. Holding on with all his strength, he made the mistake of looking down only to discover he was fifteen hundred feet from the ground below. He immediately looked toward the sky. The man was only twenty feet from where he had fallen.

"Help! Help! Is anybody there?" he yelled.

To the man's surprise he heard a booming voice respond, "I am here, and I will save you if you believe in me."

"I believe! I believe!" the man yelled back.

"If you believe me, let go of the branch and then I will save you."

The man paused, and then looked down at the ground below. Seeing the valley below, he looked back up and shouted, "Is there anybody else up there?"

This story illustrates the challenge that all of us face from time to time in our journeys of faith. Like the booming voice in the story, God promises to redeem, restore, and renew us. He even gives us the promise of heaven. All we have to do is let go of our own branches and trust in Him. Yet letting go can be hard!

The good news is that God can be trusted not only for who He is and what He has done, but also for what He will do. When you fix your hope on the promises of God, you find rest for your soul. When you place your hope in God, your strength is renewed.

All of us have questions and doubts regarding some of the things we see and encounter in this world, but God's promises are true. He will accomplish His will. He will fulfill His promises. And you can trust in Him.

1. *Have you ever felt as if you were hanging from a cliff, but God just asked you to trust Him? If so, describe. What was the outcome?*

2. *Are there any cliffs that you feel like you're hanging from right now? If so, explain.*

3. *Who is the first person you call when you're hanging from a cliff?*

4. Read **Isaiah 54:10**. What does this verse reveal about God's love for you even when you feel as if you're hanging from a cliff?

5. In the following chart, match the Scripture with the promise of God.

Bible Passage	God's Promise
Deuteronomy 33:12	When you lie down, you will not be afraid; when you lie down, your sleep will be sweet.
Psalm 4:8	The name of the Lord is a strong tower; the righteous run it to it and are safe.
Proverbs 1:33	Let the beloved of the Lord rest secure in Him, for he shields them all day long.
Proverbs 3:24	I will like down and sleep in peace, for you alone, O Lord, make me dwell in safety.
Proverbs 18:10	But whoever listens to me will live in safety and be at ease, without the fear of harm.

6. *Of the promises of God listed in the chart on the previous page, which is most meaningful to you? Why?*

7. *Read **Psalm 18:2**. What descriptions of God are listed in this verse? In what ways do those descriptions comfort you in your cliff-hanging moments?*

8. *In what ways is God asking you to trust Him and rest in Him even more through this study?*

Digging Deeper

God does not promise that trials will not come, but that He will be with you through every one of them. Read **Isaiah 43:2**. In what ways have you found this verse to be true in your own life? Explain. What keeps you holding on to God when you want to give up?

> *The truth is that you can trust God not only for who He is and what He has done, but also for what He will do!*

Ponder and Pray

The opening Scripture for this lesson comes from **Revelation 22:20**, "Yes, I am coming soon." What do you look forward to most in heaven? What gives you the most hope when you think about Jesus' return?

Bonus Activity

During the upcoming week, review the lessons in this study. Do any themes jump out to you regarding what God is trying to say to you through the questions, discussions, and Scriptures? How has this study changed the way you view the concept of rest? Consider sharing your responses with a friend, a family member, or even the author—her contact information is in the back of the study.

Leader's Guide

Each chapter begins with an illustration and an icebreaker question intended to help the women in your group relax and join in the discussion. There isn't a "right" answer to any of these warm-up questions, so everyone can participate without fear of giving a wrong response. Try to include everyone in this part of the discussion to help everyone feel comfortable and become involved in the subject matter.

Eight discussion questions guide you through the content of the chapter. When you ask one of these questions, be sure to give your group plenty of time to think and don't be surprised if they grow silent temporarily. This is fairly common in discussion groups, and the leader who gives the group ample time to reflect will find they will open up and talk. To help you stay on track, this guide identifies questions intended to draw out opinions and provides information for questions aimed at more specific answers.

The highlighted box in the study states the main point of the chapter and corresponds to the **Focus** in the guide.

Digging Deeper is for those who want to do more thinking or digging in God's Word. This part is optional for discussion, but we hope you will want to go a little deeper in your study.

Ponder and Pray offers a great way to wrap up your study by reflecting on the opening Scripture. It's an opportunity for additional thoughts for reflection and prayer.

Bonus Activity provides an opportunity to take an aspect of what you learned and place it into practice.

The Speed of Life

Chapter 1: The Stress Test

> **Focus:** *The truth is that no matter how overworked or overscheduled you may feel, God desires to restore you. Your desire for rest will never match God's desire to give you rest. He longs to renew you!*

1. *Answers may vary. Fast food and eating out save time on cooking and cleanup. Carpooling can save time on driving. If it's affordable, hiring outside help can cut down on the time need to repair the home, care for the lawn, or clean the house.*

2. *Answers may vary and some may even be humorous. Sometimes learning how to operate a new time-saving device is about as quick and easy as learning a new language!*

3. *Answers will vary. Sources of stress may include work, deadlines, and finding balance in life. Stress may result from unresolved conflict in relationships, an inability to say "no" or a*

struggle to get organized. Stress may also be the result of the needs and demands that stack up in daily life.

4. *Jesus traveled with His disciples as they went to Capernaum. He taught in the synagogue. He cast out an evil spirit. He .traveled to the home of His disciples where He healed a woman. Then He spent his evening healing the sick and demon-possessed. The Scripture reveals that the whole town gathered at His door. He silenced the evil spirits.*

5. *Finding solitary time to get away and pray was crucial to Jesus' life. It gave Jesus focused time to connect with God and ask for wisdom, guidance, and strength. It gave Jesus time to discover His Father's perspective on the matters at hand. And it gave Jesus time to remember that His identity was found in God—not in what He did.*

6. *Answers will vary, but getting away to pray is important because it allows us to get a heavenly perspective on the issues at hand. Rather than responding to situations and people out of our own earthly perspective or emotional reaction, we can seek God to discover His perspective of the matter—which is filled with love, grace, and wisdom. Getting away to pray also strengthens us—physically, emotionally, and spiritually.*

7. *Answers will vary and hopefully challenge participants to share from their own life and spiritual journey.*

8. *Answers will vary. Often the busyness that creates the stress prevents us from getting away to pray and do the very thing that helps remove stress. Yet that makes it all the more important.*

Chapter 2: The Benefits of Rest

> **Focus:** The truth is that rest restores and renews our bodies, minds, and spirits. Rest is a physical reminder that we are not in control of everything and at the end of the day, we are not the ones who have to hold it all together. That's God's job.

1. Answers will vary, but this icebreaker question is designed to allow participants to share from their own experiences.

2. Again, answers will vary, but some unhealthy alternatives include excess caffeine, sugar, as well as prescription and over-the-counter medication.

3. Answers will vary, but most people notice a chance in their physical health, mental capacity, emotional well-being, and spiritual life.

4. Life, food, drink, body, and clothing.

5. What's truly important is seeking God's kingdom and righteousness first and foremost. When we place God as the center of lives, then we are better equipped and prepared to respond to the world around us as He designed. You will always need food, water, and clothing, but they do not have to be the aim of your life. God can be your focus, and you can rest knowing that God is your ultimate Provider.

6. The psalmist has an attitude of humility. He recognizes his own limitations and lack of understanding. He acknowledges that God, alone, is the only One who knows all.

7. The psalmist chooses to "still and quiet" his soul.

8. Answers will vary, but learning to "still and quiet" your soul may mean making time to pray, sit quietly with God, study the Scripture, worship, memorize the Bible, or do an activity where the focus is solely on God. A "still and quiet" soul is better prepared to prayerfully handle conflict, interruptions, and the issues that surprise us every day.

Chapter 3: Know Your Season

Focus: The truth is that in every season of life—including our spiritual life—God does things within us that can't be done in any other season. No matter what season you're in, there's something to celebrate when it comes to what God is doing in you.

1. Answers will vary. This icebreaker question is designed to get participants talking and reflecting on some of their favorite activities during the year—from picking wildflower bouquets to the crunch of walking on fall leaves to winter sports.

2. Answers will vary. This question is designed to help participants make the link between the yearly seasons and the seasons of life.

3. *Answers will vary. Participants may feel like their spiritual life is budding with new growth and possibilities. They may sense steady growth or even a harvest of answered prayers. Or they may sense a long, hard, dark winter of wondering where God is. No matter what season a person is in, they can rest assured that God is with them and He is faithful.*

4. *Ecclesiastes 3:2—born and die.*
   Ecclesiastes 3:2—plant and uproot.
   Ecclesiastes 3:3—kill and heal.
   Ecclesiastes 3:3—tear down and build.
   Ecclesiastes 3:4—weep and laugh.
   Ecclesiastes 3:4—mourn and dance.
   Ecclesiastes 3:5—scatter and gather.
   Ecclesiastes 3:5—embrace and refrain.
   Ecclesiastes 3:6—search and give up.
   Ecclesiastes 3:6—keep and throw away.
   Ecclesiastes 3:7—tear and mend.
   Ecclesiastes 3:7—silent and speak.
   Ecclesiastes 3:8—love and hate.
   Ecclesiastes 3:8—war and peace.

5. *All of us prefer some seasons over others. They're more enjoyable, relaxing, or pleasant. Even in those seasons we don't like or enjoy, God is still at work. Often in the most difficult seasons, God is doing the deepest work in our lives.*

6. *Knowing your season removes the burden of false expectations. Just as spring is not the time to harvest, winter is not the time to expect strong, steady, tangible growth. When we recognize the season, we can respond to what God is doing in our life.*

7. There's a tendency during the busy seasons of life to skip rest, but that's often when we need it most. While the commandment to obey the Sabbath is simple, this addendum reminds us that even when life is busiest, we must still take time to rest.

8. Answers will vary. It's important to make time to rest for our bodies, minds, souls, and spirits to renew and recover. During our busiest times it's easy to be distracted from our relationship with God and treat work as if it is our god.

Applying the Breaks

Chapter 4: The Gift of Sabbath

> **Focus:** The truth is that the Sabbath is a gift from God. The Sabbath reminds us that time is holy. The Sabbath asks us to put the breaks on a busy schedule and take time to rest our souls, reorder our worlds, and realign ourselves with God.

1. Answers will vary, but if you go too long without rest and finally take time to rest, there's often a sense of "what do I do now?" The quiet and stillness can actually become uncomfortable. We may be tempted to keep moving or keep going because that's more familiar. Yet God does not want us to become strangers to the rest He gives us.

2. *Answers will vary, and there's no correct answer to this question. There does seem to be a healthy pattern in taking off one day a week to rest and remember God.*

3. *The Sabbath is not something to be legalistic about. If a person is unable in a certain season of life not to be able to take a day off a week, maybe the person can take off a half day or two half days. With prayer and creativity, the practice of Sabbath can still be enjoyed and honored.*

4. *Answers will vary, but keeping the Sabbath is linked to setting apart a day for God. When we cease from our work, then we are better able to focus on the work God is doing in our lives. Our focus shifts from ourselves to God.*

5. *This passage highlights that everyone needs rest. No one is immune. When we choose to rest and keep a Sabbath, it often creates a desire for others to follow suit. The Sabbath is seen as something to be treasured, enjoyed, and even celebrated—not just by individuals but as a community.*

6. *Jesus was highlighting the idea that many who were keeping the Sabbath had actually become enslaved to it. The Sabbath is not designed to be a burden—an added list of rules and restrictions—but to set us free to rest and embrace a deeper relationship with God.*

7. *Answers will vary. Whenever the Sabbath becomes legalistic, it will naturally be seen more as a burden than a gift.*

8. *Answers will vary, but this question is designed so participants can share the gift and beauty of the Sabbath with each other.*

Chapter 5: The Power of Margins

> **Focus:** *The truth is that when we build margins into our lives, then we give more opportunities for God to be at work within us as well as in the lives of those around us.*

1. *Answers will vary, but many people are tempted to live life as if their glass was completely filled or overflowing.*

2. *Margins are important because they give us grace, energy, time, and strength to handle the unexpected. They also provide much needed downtime and rest. Margins allow us to make sure we make time to be with God and the busyness of life doesn't get the best of us. People are tempted to live life without margins for a variety of reasons. Living with margins takes time, planning, and learning to say "no." It means establishing healthy boundaries and coming to terms with your own limitations. The pace of our modern world often places us on the fast track to busyness and maxing out every possible moment.*

3. *Answers will vary.*

4. *He makes them lie down in green pastures, leads them beside quiet waters, restores their souls, guides in paths of righteousness.*

5. *Answers will vary. A spiritual retreat, Sunday afternoon nap, extended time of prayer, or even a vacation can help us "lie down" and rest.*

6. *Answers will vary, but most people will agree busyness and lack of margins can prevent us from enjoying the life God has for us.*

7. *When we have margins, we have time and space to be more attentive to what God has for us in our schedules, daily life, and relationships.*

8. *Answers will vary, but some participants may need to cut back on activities, reschedule their weeks, or be more intentional about scheduling downtime.*

Chapter 6: The Fine Art of Saying "No"

Focus: *The truth is that while saying "no" can be difficult, it's one of the best things you can learn to do. When you learn to say "no," you open up the door to say "yes" to other things—including rest, healthy boundaries, and a more balanced life.*

1. *This icebreaker question is designed to encourage participants to reflect on the common situations that make it difficult to say "no." Sometimes it's difficult to say "no" to specific family or friend or work requests. Sometimes it's difficult to say "no" to spur-of-the-moment requests. Often guilt and fear of rejection can compound the difficulty in saying "no."*

2. *Answers will vary.*

3. *Answers will vary. Responses such as, "I can't commit to that right now," "My plate is already full," "No—but thank you for thinking of me," are some common answers.*

4. *God is like a shepherd. He is our Guide and Counselor. He ultimately knows what is best for us. When we take time to inquire of God, we may sense peace about getting involved in something new or we may sense the need to say "no." When we place every opportunity before God, we are better to able to spend our time and energy on the things that are truly important.*

5. *Answers will vary.*

6. *In 1 Chronicles 14:10, the Lord told David to attack the Philistines and that God would hand them over to David. In 1 Chronicles 14:14–15, David inquired of God again, but this time God gave very specific instructions on how to handle the situation. David's arm was to circle around the Philistines and attack them at a specific location—in front of the balsam trees— as well as a specific time—when they could hear the sound of the Philistines marching in the tops of the balsam trees. By obeying God's specific instructions, David's army defeated the Philistines.*

7. *The passage reveals that it's important to inquire of God and recognize that the answer God gives us will differ based on the situation. Sometimes God will just tell us to "go" like He did David, but other times God will have specific instructions on how we should "go," when we should "go," and even if we should "go."*

8. *Answers will vary. Participants should gently be encouraged to prayerfully consider this question.*

Rest as a Lifestyle

Chapter 7: Your Home, Your Sanctuary

Focus: *The truth is that your home can be a sanctuary, a place of rest and renewal not just for your soul, but for those who visit as well.*

1. *Answers will vary, but the most meaningful thing that a visitor says about a home usually isn't about décor, size, or furniture— it's about the atmosphere of a home. The most meaningful comments usually reflect on the peacefulness, warmth, joy, or restful nature of the home.*

2. *Answers will vary.*

3. *Answers will vary.*

4. *Answers will vary, but when we recognize that our home really belongs to God, then we are better able to give our whole selves to Him.*

5. *Answers will vary, but simple things like playing worship music, making Scripture or Bibles available, or keeping Christian books throughout the house can be gentle, thoughtful reminders and encouragers to pursue a relationship with God. In addition, prayer, spiritual conversations, and sharing your own story can encourage others.*

6. You can have a perfect home and serve the perfect meal, but if your attitude is unbecoming, it will undermine your efforts at hospitality. Real hospitality is about our hearts—not the food, décor, or even neatness of the home.

7. Love must be sincere. Hate what is evil; cling to what is good. Be devoted to one another in brotherly love. Honor one another above yourselves. Never be lacking in zeal, but keep your spiritual fervor, serving the Lord. Be joyful in hope, patient in affliction, and faithful in prayer. Share with God's people who are in need. Practice hospitality. Following the instructions in Romans 12:9–13 creates peace in our hearts that is contagious. When we love and honor, practice patience and prayer, and share with others, we find rest for our souls as we live in peace with others.

8. Answers will vary.

Chapter 8: Discovering the Secret Place

Focus: The truth is that God desires for you to abide in Him and discover Him as your refuge. When you abide in the secret place of God, you can't help but discover rest for your soul.

1. Answers will vary, but hopefully participants will be able to think of times when they felt close to God in the more mundane activities of life.

2. *Answers will vary, but God wants to be involved in all of our lives, every moment. Sometimes we have a tendency to turn to God in the more exciting or stressful moments, but God wants to have a relationship with us all day, every day—no activity or moment is too small or insignificant.*

3. *Answers will vary, but usually that moment in life when God is a secret hiding place makes God all the more real to us. At those times, our faith grows and we discover that God is one to be trusted.*

4. *Answers will vary.*

5. *Answers will vary.*

6. *When we abide in God, we can bear fruit. Apart from God, we cannot bear lasting fruit. In fact, the Scripture says we can't do anything on our own. If we don't abide in God, then, like a branch, we wither and die.*

7. *Answers will vary.*

8. *Answers will vary.*

Chapter 9: Moments of Retreat

Focus: *The truth is that sometimes you have to retreat in order to advance. Retreats—times when you get away from the busy demands of everyday life—allow you to recharge physically, emotionally and spiritually.*

1. *Answers will vary. Generally, retreats allow us to refresh, refocus, and renew. They allow us to connect with God in a special way.*

2. *Answers will vary. Many people don't think about taking a mini-retreat. They think about larger, longer getaways. But you don't have to leave town to have a retreat. A morning of prayer, an afternoon of rest, or an evening of solitude can go a long way to helping you reconnect with God.*

3. *Moments of retreat provide opportunity to regain perspective, relax, and rejuvenate. They allow us to maintain a healthier rhythm in life.*

4. *Answers will vary. Being still can be incredibly difficult if you're used to constantly living on the go. Yet being still reminds us that God is God and we are not.*

5. *Answers will vary.*

6.

Bible Passage	Where Jesus went to retreat
Matthew 14:13	He withdrew to a lonely place such as the wilderness.
Matthew 15:21	The Spirit led him into the desert.
Mark 3:7	He withdrew by boat to a solitary place.
Luke 5:16	He withdrew to the region of Tyre and Sidon.
Mark 1:12	He withdrew with His disciples to a lake.

7. *Answers will vary, but Jesus, too, needed moments of retreat to reconnect with the Father. There isn't necessarily a specific pattern to the places, methods, or style of retreat, but what's clear is that Jesus went away regularly. Sometimes Jesus withdrew alone. Sometimes He withdrew with His disciples. He didn't go to one particular place consistently, but He still found a place to go wherever He was.*

8. *Jesus prayed. Prayer is important to moments of retreat because it allows us to connect with God, lay our concerns and cares before Him, and listen for an answer. Through prayer, we can connect with God and love on Him just as we are loved by Him.*

Resting in God

Chapter 10: Resting in Who He Is

> **Focus:** *The truth is that hiding God's Word in your heart helps you to know God even better! And as you know God, you discover Him as your source of joy, strength, peace, and rest.*

1. *Answers will vary, but memorizing Scripture can help transform the way we think and direct our hearts back to God. At times, Scriptures will pop into our mind and offer instruction, encouragement, direction, and guidance when we need it most.*

2. Through the Bible we get to know God. The Bible is like a love letter from God. As we study it, we get to know Him—the Author and Creator.

3. Answers will vary.

4. Psalm 19:8—As we study God's Word, we find that it is a source of joy and life.

Psalm 103:1—As we study God's Word, we are better able to worship Him.

Psalm 119:11—As we study God's Word, we are better able to avoid sin.

Psalm 119:40—As we study God's Word, we find safety and protection.

5. Answers will vary.

6.

Name of God	Scripture Reference	Meaning of Name of God
Yahweh Jireh (Yireh)	Genesis 22:14	The Lord will provide.
Yahweh Nissi	Exodus 17:15	The Lord is my banner.
Yahweh Shalom	Judges 6:24	The Lord is peace.
Yahweh Sabbaoth	1 Samuel 1:3	The Lord Almighty or the Lord of Hosts.
Yahweh Ro'i	Psalm 23:1	The Lord is my shepherd.
Yahweh Elohim Israel	Isaiah 17:6	The Lord, the God of Israel.
Yahweh Tsidkenu	Jeremiah 23:6	The Lord Our Righteousness.

7. *Answers will vary, but knowing the meanings of God's names provides peace, grace, strength, and restoration, among many other things.*

8. *Answers will vary but include studying the Word, spending time in prayer and worship, as well as spending time with other believers.*

Chapter 11: Resting in What He's Done

> **Focus:** *The truth is that when you know God and what He has done, it's easier to step into the wheelbarrow and rest in Him no matter what journey you might be facing.*

1. *Just like the man in the audience, it's easy to say we believe, but real faith requires that we trust God, not just in word, but in deed. That can be scary, but the good news is that God is trustworthy.*

2. *Answers will vary.*

3. *Just as you wouldn't want to step into the wheelbarrow of a tightrope walker you didn't know, it's hard to trust that which you don't know about. That's why knowing what God has done is so important to strengthening your faith and resting in Him.*

4. *Numbers 23:19: This verse reveals that God does not lie. He is a God of truth and can be trusted.*

   Deuteronomy 4:31: This verse reveals that God is merciful. He is also true to His Word.

Deuteronomy 7:9: This verse reveals that God is faithful. His love is based on a covenant, a solid commitment, to us.

2 Peter 3:9: This verse reveals that God is patient. He does not want to see anyone perish but instead wants to see everyone saved.

5. *Answers will vary.*

6. *Psalm 119:89–90: God's Word is eternal and stands firm in the heavens. His faithfulness continues through all generations.*

   Isaiah 46:11: God can use all things to fulfill His purpose. What He promises and plans, He does.

   Isaiah 54:10: No matter what happens, God's love is steadfast. His covenant of peace will not be removed. God has compassion on us.

7. *Answers will vary.*

8. *Answers will vary.*

Chapter 12: Resting in What He Will Do

> **Focus:** *The truth is that you can trust God not only for who He is and what He has done, but also for what He will do!*

1. *Answers will vary, but this icebreaker question is designed to help participants recall a challenging time in life when they discovered God to be faithful and true.*

101

2. *Answers will vary, but the "cliffs" of life take many forms, including marital conflict, unresolved hurt, financial challenges, health complications, life transitions, and many more. At those moments, God invites us to call out to Him in prayer and trust Him with everything.*

3. *Answers will vary, but you may be tempted to call out to a spouse, family member, friend, or counselor. God invites us to call out to Him first.*

4. *God's love is secure and firm. He is with you in every situation and His promises are trustworthy.*

5.

Bible Passage	God's Promise
Deuteronomy 33:12	When you lie down, you will not be afraid; when you lie down, your sleep will be sweet.
Psalm 4:8	The name of the Lord is a strong tower; the righteous run into it and are safe.
Proverbs 1:33	Let the beloved of the Lord rest secure in Him, for He shields them all day long.
Proverbs 3:24	I will lie down and sleep in peace, for you alone, O Lord, make me dwell in safety.
Proverbs 18:10	But whoever listens to Me will live in safety and be at ease, without the fear of harm.

6. *Answers will vary.*

7. *The Lord is a rock, fortress, deliverer, horn of salvation, and stronghold.*

8. *Answers will vary.*

About the Author

Margaret Feinberg is an author and speaker who offers a refreshing perspective on faith and the Bible. She has written more than a dozen books including *The Organic God* and *God Whispers*. She also wrote the Women of Faith Bible Study *Overcoming Fear*. Margaret is a popular speaker at women's events, luncheons, and retreats as well as national conferences including Catalyst, LeadNow, Fusion, and the National Pastor's Conference.

She lives in Lakewood, Colorado, in the shadow of the Rockies with her 6'8" husband, Leif. When she's not writing and traveling, she loves hiking, shopping, blogging, laughing, and drinking skinny vanilla lattes with her girlfriends. But some of her best days are spent communicating with her readers.

So if you want to put a smile on her face, go ahead and write her!

Margaret@margaretfeinberg.com

www.margaretfeinberg.com

www.margaretfeinberg.blogspot.com

Tag her on Facebook or follow her on twitter

www.twitter.com/mafeinberg

Additional Resources

What Shall We Study Next?

Women of Faith® has numerous study guides out right now
that will draw you closer to God.

Living Above Worry and Stress

*Consider the lilies, how they grow: they neither toil
nor spin; and yet I say to you, even Solomon in all
his glory was not arrayed like one of these. If then
God so clothes the grass, which today is in the field
and tomorrow is thrown into the oven, how much
more will He clothe you, O you of little faith?*

Luke 12:27–28, NKJV

The words echo back to us from years gone by. We first learned it in a Vacation Bible School one summer or from a dear Sunday school teacher—the voice of Jesus calling us to consider the lilies. The lesson was a simple one: don't worry. If God would give the flowers such pretty petals, dressing them more grandly than wealthy King Solomon could manage, He will provide for our needs too.

Unfortunately, the call to consider the lilies is left on a dusty shelf somewhere. It's probably right next to the old plea to stop and smell the roses. We're too busy for stopping. We're too rushed for consideration. Our "to do" lists are long. Our day timers are booked. Our time is money. We can't keep up.

We are busy people. We have responsibilities at work. We have responsibilities at home. We have responsibilities at church. We have responsibilities at school. We have responsibilities within our communities. We care for the needs of our parents, our husbands, our children, our siblings, our employers, our closest friends. Most days, it is more than we can handle. Our hearts are overwhelmed. We are stressed out. We are worried. We dread tomorrow.

In the midst of all this everyday turmoil, our hearts long for a place of peace. We know God has promised us rest. We know He says we don't have to worry about tomorrow. He promised to calm our fears. Yet we barely have time to whisper a prayer, let alone study our Bibles. If you have been struggling, come. Let's take a little time to explore the Scriptures, and find some practical guidelines for laying aside our fears, our worry, and even our stress. You really can discover a place of peace.

Living in Jesus

Those who become Christians become new persons.
They are not the same anymore, for the old life is
gone. A new life has begun!

2 Corinthians 5:17, NLT

Have you ever read books just to escape the never-ending dullness of everyday life? Through the chapters of some paperback, we experience the shadows of an existence that seems more interesting, more exciting, more appealing than what our own day has to offer. Damsels find unfailing love, sleuths seek out elusive clues, strangers form unlikely alliances, adventurers cross unfamiliar terrains, and they all live happily ever after. In comparison, we feel boring, listless, and wistful.

Little do we realize that as believers, we have been ushered into a life that rivals the plot of any mere story! We have become leading ladies in a thrilling tale of epic proportions. There's something for everyone: combat, romance, intrigue, drama, rescue, duplicity, character development, action, adventure, complex subplots, moral dilemmas, sacrifice, tear jerking, subtle humor, slapstick, subterfuge, betrayal, showdowns, discovery, unexpected twists, irony, paradise, and a happy ending.

The Christian life is vibrant, mysterious, and beautiful. In a word— sensational! Open your eyes to the wonder of a life knit with the divine. Jesus has called you, chosen you, changed you. Your life is caught up with His, transformed into something altogether new. Jesus is your intimate friend—familiar, inseparable, precious. He has called you His beloved, and made you fantastic promises. Your life is a never-ending story that will continue to unfold throughout eternity.

All because of what you are *in Him*.

Adventurous Prayer: Talking with God

Prayer is reaching out to touch Someone—namely,
your Creator. In the process, He touches you.

BARBARA JOHNSON

What's the big deal about prayer? We know we should all do it more often, take it more seriously, and give it more time—but we don't. Does that mean that prayer is optional? After all, some of the other spiritual disciplines seem pretty outdated, like fasting and solitude. Who has time for that? That kind of stuff is for monks, nuns, and pastors. We've gotten along okay without it.

So, does prayer fit into the *non*-essentials of the Christian walk? Prayer must be that "in case of emergency" last-resort kind of spiritual tool. Right?

Shame on you!

Prayer isn't some kind of requirement for believers. It is a privilege! You have the ear of the Divine. Prayer is our path to the adventure of building a relationship with our Savior.

God knows what's going on in your life. The Creator of all that is stoops to hear the lisping of toddlers. The Sustainer of every living thing hears the groans and sighs of the aging. He is aware of every thought, every choice, every move you make—but He is waiting for you to turn to Him and tell Him about it.

God listens to you. He will answer you.

THE COMPLETE WOMEN OF FAITH®
STUDY GUIDE SERIES

To find these and other inspirational products visit your local Christian retailer.

THOMAS NELSON
Since 1798

WOMEN OF FAITH
DEVOTIONAL JOURNAL

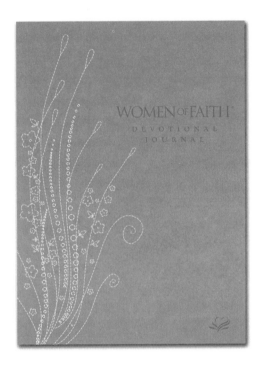

*T*he *Women of Faith Devotional Journal*
speaks directly to the subject of God's infinite grace. Filled with
stirring quotes and uplifting Scripture, this journal is the ideal
addition to any devotional time.

- SCRIPTURE VERSES HIGHLIGHT WISDOM FOR DAILY LIFE

- YOUR FAVORITE WOMEN OF FAITH SPEAKERS' ENLIGHTENING
  THOUGHTS ON GRACE

- PLENTY OF WRITING SPACE TO RECORD DREAMS, HOPES,
  AND PERSONAL REFLECTIONS

WOMEN OF FAITH

THOMAS NELSON
Since 1798